FOOTROT FLATS

one

BY *Murray Ball*

SPLUK! SPLUK!

ORIN BOOKS

MURRAY BALL

Born Feilding 1939

Educated in New Zealand, Australia and South Africa.

Ex Junior All Black, N.Z. trialist, journalist, menswear salesman, dodgem car attendant, freezing worker, amateur farm hand, coin machine operator, author and school teacher.

Spent five years in Britain during which time he drew freelance cartoons, illustrated children's comics and drew a regular cartoon feature "Stanley" for "Punch" magazine.

Returned to New Zealand and now runs a cow, calf, three ewes, a ram, five lambs, a flock of hens, a rooster, some ducks, two geese, two cats, a multitude of insects and three children on his four-acre ranch in Gisborne.

In this he is aided by his wife Pam, who is English and does the odd jobs like looking after the house, keeping the accounts, controlling the kids, feeding the animals, ruling up his drawings, rubbing out pencil lines, filing, cooking, digging the garden, planting the vegetables and worrying about the lambs. She refuses to mow the lawns.

At present he is drawing "Footrot Flats" daily and Sunday, which appears in over 70 newspapers and magazines around Australia and New Zealand; and "Stanley" which appears in the Sydney "Sun Herald", and "Listener", Wellington, New Zealand.

Likes Greek music and spaghetti with red wine.

I gotta hand it to Wal, he isn't pushy. Nope, if there's a bull to be moved, he lets me do it. If someone has to have first taste of Cooch's toad and enunga fritters, he lets me do it. If there's a book to be started and there's footy on television, he lets me do it.

Well, as it happens, he has got just the right joker for the job. I happen to know the Footrot Flat weirdos better than most. I have ridden on, fallen under, been trampled by, rolled over and been butted, kicked, savaged, licked, pecked or hurled by most of them at one time or another. And there is no better way of getting to know a person than to have actually been inside their gumboot, I always think.

So, in the next few pages, I'm going to tell you a bit about the Footrot Flats mob— starting with probably the toughest, most powerful, interesting and yet most modest of them all . . .

First published in Australia September 1978. World copyright. All rights reserved. © Murray Ball 1976-78. Published by Orin Books, P.O. Box 89, St. Kilda West, Victoria, Australia 3182. Reprinted November 1978, February 1979, March 1980, October 1980, March 1981, April 1982.

Printed by The Dominion Press, North Blackburn, Victoria.

ISSN 0156-6172

Syndicated internationally outside New Zealand by Inter Continental Features, P.O. Box 89, St. Kilda West, Vic. Australia 3182.

FOOTROT FLATS comic strip is now appearing daily in the Brisbane COURIER MAIL, Melbourne HERALD, Sydney DAILY MIRROR, Adelaide NEWS, Perth WEST AUSTRALIAN, Launceston EXAMINER; Sydney SUNDAY TELEGRAPH, and many other newspapers around Australia too numerous to list individually.

THE DOG

[A PICTORIAL HISTORY]

EARLY DAYS

INTRODUCTION TO FARM LIFE

TRAINING TO BE AN EYE DOG

GAINING EXPERIENCE

MATURITY

WAL'

WALLACE FOOTROT CADWALLADER

Born on 26th January in Northern Manawatu.

Educated at Apiti Primary School and later Foxton Agricultural High, where he excelled at tractor reversing and rooster imitations. Established an outstanding relationship with muscovy ducks—but unfortunately failed completely with geese. Indeed he seemed to have an uncanny knack of irritating them.

He took a full part in all school activities. Displayed a promising right cross during his time in the front row of the 2nd XV, but was unable to transfer this ability to the boxing ring. He rather let the side down during the inter-school championships by throwing in the sponge which knocked the referee's glasses crooked. He was disqualified.

On leaving school, he acquired 400 acres of swamp between the Ureweras and the sea.

He is unmarried, although he has an interest in a certain Darlene (Cheeky) Hobson who works in the Ladies Hairdressers at Raupo (pop. 406).

He is a stalwart of the local rugby football team. He was a moving force in formalising the law that football boots will be worn only when more than 60 percent of both sides has a pair.

A good-humoured fellow who smiles readily. (The last time was when Cooch got his arm caught down a rabbit burrow while trying to rescue a rabbit. He laughed aloud when the rabbit bit Cooch. That was in 1974).

He has relations all over New Zealand. As a matter of fact he got me from his Aunty Dolly in Tauranga. She is a terrible woman. She attended a Royal Garden Party on a trip to London and has never recovered from the honour of treading in Corgi droppings under a Rhododendron bush. Her shoe is kept in a glass box on her colour television set. She named me.

COOCH WINDGRASS

Wal's mate, neighbour and right hand man. A beauty bloke—ask any possum, deer, rabbit, magpie or weta. The only joker I know who'd give his Jacky Howe to a slug with a sniffle.

He keeps goats and blackberry. He has a cabbage tree growing up through his verandah floor. The roots of a Puriri have pushed his house crooked. You have to climb up the floors in some places and jog down the slope in others.

The most violent act I ever saw him commit, was to spit a codlin moth from his apple out of the window.

Mind you, he's not a vegetarian. He does kill to eat. His eel and puffball stew is an acquired taste, as is his huhu grub, puha and chips. A native of the 'Flats'—his family owns two thousand acres of swamp, tussock, scrub, forest and mudflat. Wal reckons it's a crime that they don't bulldoze it flat and farm sheep instead of pipis and paua. But I reckon he's got a soft spot for old Cooch—like the rest of us.

He can catch flounder with his bare feet.

MAJOR

Wal's pig dog. Thinks he's a big wheel. Just because he's tough, strong, brave, courageous and brainy, he thinks he's better than the rest of us. Well, I'm going to show him one day. I'm working on being as brainy as him at the moment—and that tells me I shouldn't rush things. But he just better watch it, that's all!

THE GOOSE

Wal hates the goose. The goose seems to quite like Wal because it is always having a piece of him.

I get on all right with the goose. I don't get in its way and it doesn't get in my way if I see it coming in time.

THE TURKEY

My main enemy. A Bully. And like all bullies, a coward. One day I'm going to stand up to him, grab that red dangly thing on his beak and sock him right between the eyes with it. That'll show him up for the coward he is.

When I get older—after Christmas, maybe . . .

THE GOAT

Wal got him to keep the grass down. But he doesn't seem to like grass. He seems to prefer to keep the fruit trees, Wal's footy socks and Wal down.

I'm not going to say too much here as the cunning old sod is sharp enough to read it.

THEY TELL ME IT ALSO STOPS SHEEP.

GIT AWAY AROUND HIM DOG!

HE'S JOKIN', THAT'S A BLOODY BULL!

HE'S A KILLER! HOW COULD I MOVE A MONSTER LIKE THAT?

I MEAN THERE IS NO WAY I COULD MOVE IT — NO WAY!

THWAK!

WHY DIDN'T I THINK OF THAT?

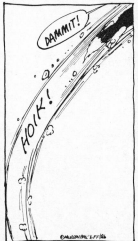

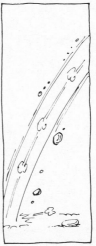

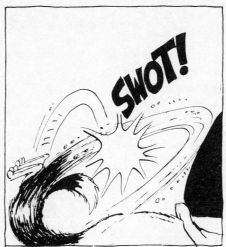

theEND